Facing Mighty Fears
About Baddies and Villains

Dr. Dawn's Mini Books About Mighty Fears
By Dawn Huebner, PhD
Illustrated by Liza Stevens
Helping children ages 6–10 live happier lives

Facing Mighty Fears
About Health
ISBN 978 1 78775 928 2
eISBN 978 1 78775 927 5

Facing Mighty Fears
About Trying New Things
ISBN 978 1 78775 950 3
eISBN 978 1 78775 951 0

Facing Mighty Fears
About Throwing Up
ISBN 978 1 78775 925 1
eISBN 978 1 78775 926 8

Facing Mighty Fears
About Animals
ISBN 978 1 78775 946 6
eISBN 978 1 78775 947 3

Watch for future titles in the
Dr. Dawn's Mini Books About Mighty Fears series.

Facing Mighty Fears About Baddies and Villains

Dawn Huebner, PhD

Illustrated by Liza Stevens

Jessica Kingsley Publishers
London and Philadelphia

First published in Great Britain in 2023 by Jessica Kingsley Publishers
An Hachette Company

1

Copyright © Dawn Huebner, PhD 2023
Illustrations copyright © Liza Stevens 2023

Front cover image source: Liza Stevens.

A CIP catalogue record for this title is available from the
British Library and the Library of Congress

ISBN 978 1 83997 462 5
eISBN 978 1 83997 463 2

Printed and bound in Great Britain by TJ Books Limited

Jessica Kingsley Publishers' policy is to use papers that are natural,
renewable, and recyclable products and made from wood grown in
sustainable forests. The logging and manufacturing processes are expected
to conform to the environmental regulations of the country of origin.

Jessica Kingsley Publishers
Carmelite House
50 Victoria Embankment
London EC4Y 0DZ

www.jkp.com

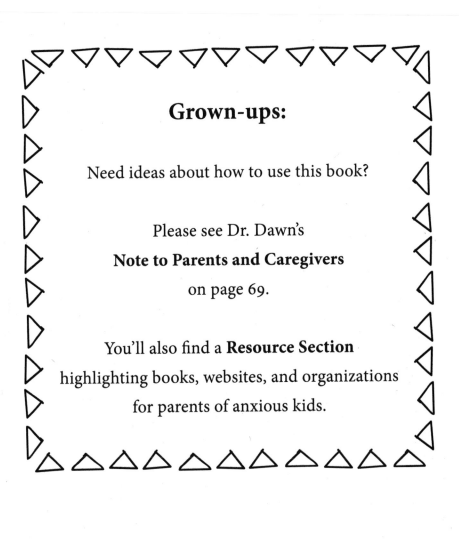

Grown-ups:

Need ideas about how to use this book?

Please see Dr. Dawn's
Note to Parents and Caregivers
on page 69.

You'll also find a **Resource Section**
highlighting books, websites, and organizations
for parents of anxious kids.

Most kids like goodies.

If someone offered you a goody, I bet you'd say,

And pop that goody into your mouth.

You might:

CRUNCH IT

slurp it

nibble, nibble, nibble it

suck it

savor it

CHEW IT

GOBBLE IT

And then you'd be ready for more.

Goodies are like that. They are so **GOOD**.

The opposite of goody is baddy.

But baddies aren't food. They are characters and people who do mean scary things.

MONSTER

ROBBER

witch

VAMPIRE

bad guy

kidnapper

INTRUDER

ghost

DOLL THAT COMES TO LIFE

ogre

devil

ZOMBIE

TROLL

villain

Some baddies are real—actual people doing actual hurtful things.

Other baddies are pretend—characters in books, games, movies, and stories friends tell, even though the baddy never took an actual breath and isn't real at all.

Most people are afraid of baddies.

That makes sense. Baddies do hurtful things, so of course people feel afraid.

If you are reading this book, you might be a child who wishes there was no such thing as baddies.

You might not want to hear about them, read about them, watch them, or even think about them.

Or maybe you do like hearing about baddies, but later it isn't much fun because remembering makes you feel scared.

There might be a particular baddy that frightens you.

Maybe you saw that baddy on a show or encountered it in a game.

Maybe you read about the baddy in a book.

Maybe someone told you about the baddy, or you dreamed him or her up in your own mind.

You might remember how you first learned about the baddy, and you might not. Either way, you keep thinking about the baddy now.

Thoughts about the baddy might make it hard for you to walk around your house or stay in a room alone.

They might make you ask if windows and doors are locked, and make you want a parent to stay with you while you are falling asleep.

Your parents probably tell you that your house is safe. They probably say that the baddies you fear aren't anywhere near you. But if you are like most kids, that doesn't really help.

Thoughts about baddies are too **sticky**.

What does that mean, for a thought to be sticky?

Well, you know what "sticky" means, right?

Sticky means clingy. When you touch a sticky thing, it stays on your finger— like glue, or honey, or sticky tape.

So, a sticky thought is a thought that stays in your brain. It holds on, even though you don't want it to.

When you have a sticky thought—about baddies, for example—and someone says,

Baddies aren't real. Don't worry about them.

It's like they're telling you to just spit that thought out of your head.

You try to spit it out, but you can't.

The thought stays stubbornly stuck.

So, what's the solution?

Do you have to go through your whole life with sticky thoughts that scare you and make it hard to do things?

Nope.

There's a trick to getting rid of sticky thoughts. A trick thousands of kids have learned that you can learn, too.

And the best news is, you already know this trick! You just don't realize you can use it on sticky thoughts.

So, what is this trick?

Well, it has to do with something else that's sticky: **gum**.

That's right. Gum. The kind you unwrap and chew.

If you have gum at your house, and if you are allowed to chew it, you might want to get a piece now, but don't unwrap it quite yet.

And if not, simply imagine your favorite kind of gum. Maybe it's mint. Or grape. Or cinnamon. Or bubble gum.

FUN FACT
Unusual flavors of gum include pickle, bacon, wasabi, meatball, soap, mint chocolate chip ice cream, foie gras (duck liver), banana, eggnog, black pepper, popcorn, cola, frank-and-beans, licorice, and clove.

FUN FACT
The most popular flavor of gum is spearmint, followed closely by peppermint.

If you are imagining gum, picture someone handing you a stick or a blob or a length of it.

FUN FACT
Gum comes in many forms, including stick, square, tablet, coated pellet, slab, ribbon, tube, and center filled.

Imagine yourself putting the gum into your mouth, and slowly bringing your teeth together.

And if you have actual gum, unwrap a piece and put it into your mouth.

What's that like, when you put a fresh piece of gum into your mouth and take your first chew?

Even if you don't have an actual piece of gum, you can imagine what that's like.

It's amazing, isn't it?

The flavor is so strong. So **pervasive**.

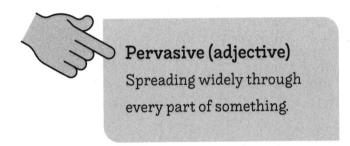

Pervasive (adjective)
Spreading widely through every part of something.

Your whole mouth gets flooded with flavor. Mint or grape or cinnamon or bubble, the flavor is absolutely everywhere.

Now imagine someone coming along, your teacher maybe, or your dentist. And that person saying,

I'm sorry. You can't be chewing gum right now. You need to spit it out.

Would that be easy or hard?

It would be hard, wouldn't it? Because the flavor is so **intense**, and you had just gotten started.

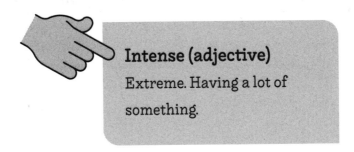

Intense (adjective)
Extreme. Having a lot of something.

Whether you are imagining this or chewing gum for real, you know that you would definitely want to keep that gum in your mouth so you could chew some more.

Okay, now imagine this.

Again, someone hands you a piece of gum—your favorite kind—and you pop it into your mouth.

Again, an explosion of flavor.

Only this time, no one interrupts you. No one tells you to spit out the gum, so you don't. Instead, you chew.

You chew.

 And you chew.

 And you chew.

 And you chew.

At first, the gum is SO GOOD. So much flavor. So delicious.

But what happens after a while?

The flavor goes away.

So then, if someone comes along and says,

It's time to spit out your gum.

That would be easy.

You'd spit it right out because your mouth would be tired of the gum anyway.

The flavor would be gone, so there would be no reason to keep it in your mouth.

FUN FACT
Most gum loses its flavor in 2 to 5 minutes.

FUN FACT
Most gum ends up in landfills, but inventors have figured out how to recycle it to make toys, phone cases, shoes, coffee cups, skateboard wheels, and rubber bins.

Which brings us back to sticky thoughts and the trick we talked about earlier.

FUN FACT

Humans are the only animals who like gum. When monkeys are given gum, they chew it only briefly, then take it out and stick it to their fur.

FUN FACT

If you ever get gum in your hair, grab some peanut butter. The oils in peanut butter separate gum from hair, so the gum will come right out. Getting the peanut butter out is another story!

Thoughts about baddies are like gum.

Not the delicious part, but the part about them being intense.

EXTREME

CONCENTRATED

POWERFUL

FIERY

STRONG

overmuch

BRUTAL

HARSH

SEVERE

fierce

When a baddy-thought comes into your brain and you try to spit it out, you can't.

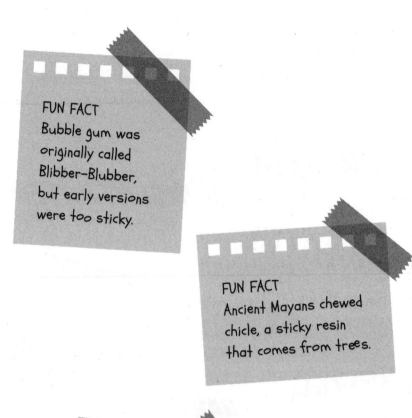

FUN FACT
Bubble gum was originally called Blibber-Blubber, but early versions were too sticky.

FUN FACT
Ancient Mayans chewed chicle, a sticky resin that comes from trees.

FUN FACT
Swedish scientists have found a 9000-year-old wad of chewing gum.

So, the trick is to remember what you do with gum.

You chew it, right?

Chewing makes the intensity go away.

It's the same with thoughts.

You can "chew" them to make the intensity go away.

The following three steps will show you how.

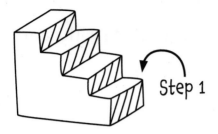

Step 1

1. Unwrap the thought and put it into your brain.

Don't wait for a baddy-thought to pop into your head. Put it there.

Reach for your baddy-thoughts. Invite them in. Think about baddies on purpose.

You can write the name of the baddy.

Write it lots of ways.

Put it in bubble letters to make a fancy poster.

Write it with your left hand, and then your right hand, and then your left hand, and then your right hand.

You can say the name of the baddy.

Say it fast and slow, in funny voices and serious voices. Pronounce the name backwards. Say it in Pig Latin.

FUN FACT
The first flavored chewing gum was made in the 1860s by John Colgan. He called it Taffy Tolu.

FUN FACT
In 1928, after lots of experimenting, an accountant named Walter Diemer created a super-stretchy gum he called Double Bubble. There was only one shade of food coloring available to him—pink. The pink bubble gum he created was such a hit we still chew it today.

You can make up a song about the baddy, complete with lyrics and music.

Or look for an app that turns spoken words into raps.

Or sing the baddy's name over and over to the tune of your favorite song.

You can use your body to make letters that spell the baddy's name:

For example, touch your chest with the fingertips of both hands, sticking your elbows out so each arm makes a loop, then bend way over sideways—that's a B.

Spread your legs wide and join your hands above your head for A.

Bend all the way down, arch your back, and grasp your ankles for D. If you were spelling baddy, you'd do this one twice.

Stand straight with your legs together and arms spread up and out for Y.

The idea is to say the baddy's name, and write the baddy's name, and hear the baddy's name, over and over again.

Use the examples you just read about or make up activities of your own.

Put the name of the baddy you think about most into your mind on purpose.

MONSTER ROBBER witch VAMPIRE INTRUDER ghost kidnapper villain devil bad guy DOLL THAT COMES TO LIFE ogre ZOMBIE TROLL

Unwrap it and begin to chew.

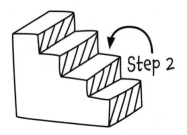

Step 2

2. Chew out the scariness.

You've put the name of the baddy into your head, and you've started to chew.

Good for you!

Remember, the first few chews are going to be **intense**.

You might want to spit your thoughts out, but it's better to keep chewing.

FUN FACT
Chewing is good
for your brain;
it increases
concentration and
focus.

FUN FACT
Michael Amato
holds the speed-
blowing record,
with 15 bubbles in
a single minute.

Set aside 15 minutes a day for chew-time.

During chew-time, you can:

Draw the baddy. You can draw them from memory or find a picture to copy. Draw them doing something mean, or make your picture funny, like the baddy sliding on a banana peel and landing—**splat**—on their bottom.

Or you can find a picture of the baddy online, print it out, and add to it—pasting on a funny bathing suit or silly hat.

You can act out the baddy going about their day.

Or ask a parent to help you conduct an interview, taking turns asking questions. You might ask your baddy-parent:

Then trade places and let your parent interview baddy-you.

You can make up a story about the baddy.

Include a real-life hero or a fictional superhero able to

tame the baddy,

or lock them up,

or transform them into someone

or something good.

Chew on baddy-thoughts with these activities or others like them for at least 15 minutes a day.

Longer, more frequent chewing will get rid of the scariness even faster.

FUN FACT
Chiclephobia is the fear of chewing gum or being around someone who is chewing gum.

FUN FACT
The first winner of the "Chomp Title" was Sue Jordan, who chewed 80 pieces of Doublemint gum for five hours. Clyde McGehee broke her record by chewing 105 sticks of Juicy Fruit for six hours. Richard Walker is the current champion, chewing 135 pieces of bubble gum over the course of eight hours.

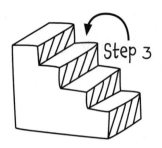

Step 3

3. Walk and chew at the same time.

After you have completed at least five 15-minute chew-times, you'll be ready to start walking and chewing at the same time.

That means you'll be thinking baddy-thoughts while doing scary-seeming things.

FUN FACT
The largest bubble blown out of someone's nose was 11 inches. But from their nose? Ick!

FUN FACT
Chad Fell holds the record for the largest hands-free bubble gum bubble, using three pieces of gum to blow a bubble over 20 inches (50 centimeters) big. That's twice the size of a basketball!

Start by making a list of the activities you've been avoiding because baddy-thoughts make them hard.

Your list might include:

Going outside alone.

Going into a room alone.

Going to bed without checking doors or locks.

Going into a dark space alone.

Going upstairs or downstairs alone.

Put your list in order from the easiest-seeming to the hardest-seeming thing.

Put a star next to the easiest-seeming thing. That's where you will begin.

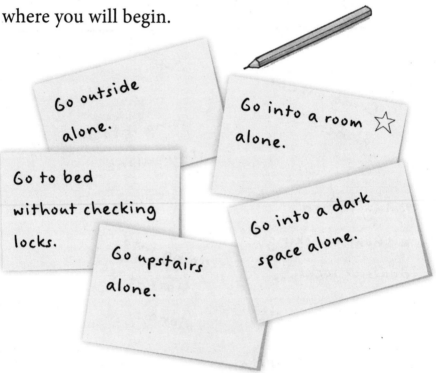

But even your "easiest" thing might seem too hard.

That's okay.

You can break any challenge into smaller steps to make it more manageable.

For example, if you are practicing going upstairs alone, you might first go halfway up with a parent standing at the bottom of the stairs.

Then go all the way up, with your parent still standing at the bottom.

Then go all the way up and do something quick, like touch a few doorknobs.

Each activity is a single chew. For example:

Chew #1 Go halfway up the stairs with a parent standing at the bottom.

Chew #2 Go all the way up with a parent standing at the bottom.

Chew #3 Go all the way up and touch three doorknobs with a parent standing at the bottom.

Chew #4 Go all the way up and touch three doorknobs while a parent stands further away.

Chew #5 Go all the way up with a parent further away. Touch every doorknob, including room doors, closet doors, and cabinet doors.

Chew #6 Go all the way up with a parent further away. Do ten Jumping Jacks in every room.

Chew #7 Go all the way up with a parent further away. Sit in a room and draw yourself playing a sport you love.

Make each chew just a tiny bit bigger, so eventually you are going up and staying alone for 15 minutes at a time.

But wait. You aren't quite done.

You need to go back through each of the steps and do them again, this time while thinking about baddies.

FUN FACT
Gum is the second most common form of litter, after cigarette butts.

FUN FACT
If you visit Bubblegum Alley in California, you will see colorful hunks of chewed-up gum covering the walls, millions of pieces left by visitors. The alley is periodically scraped and cleaned, but it always fills up again.

So, for example, you might walk up the stairs singing your baddy-rap.

Or say the name of the baddy every time you touch a doorknob.

Or draw a picture of the baddy while you are in your room alone.

The idea is to do the things you have been avoiding while thinking about the baddy on purpose.

Once you have tackled the easiest activity on your list, move to the next easiest, break it into smaller steps if needed, and do the whole thing again.

Make your way through the list of activities you've been avoiding, one activity at a time, one chew at a time.

FUN FACT
250,000 wads of gum were found stuck to Oxford Street in London.

FUN FACT
15,000 pieces of gum are spit out on the streets of Rome every day. It costs one Euro to remove each one.

FUN FACT
Singapore didn't want to deal with gum waste, so they banned gum, imposing large fines and even jail time for people caught chewing it.

At first, it might not seem like anything is happening.

Keep chewing.

chew chew chew
chew chew
chew
chew chew

Challenge yourself a little bit more, and a little bit more.

FUN FACT
There are more than 1000 varieties of gum manufactured and sold in the US.

FUN FACT
Mastika Gum is the most expensive gum in the world because it is coated with edible 22-carat gold.

Before too long, something amazing will start to happen.

The intensity of your thoughts and the scariness of them will begin to fade, just like the flavor of gum.

FUN FACT

Many scientists don't think gum should be classified as food because it contains ingredients not meant to be swallowed. But because people put gum into their mouths, the solution was to call it food with "minimal nutritional value."

MINIMAL NUTRITIONAL VALUE

Your brain will start to get bored, realizing the thoughts are just thoughts, with no power to hurt you.

BADDY

BADDY

BADDY

BADDY

BADDY

BADDY

BADDY

BADDY

You will begin to realize that you don't need to avoid the activities you were avoiding because there is nothing dangerous about them.

After all, being afraid is not the same as being in danger.

When you do the things you were avoiding, and nothing bad happens, it will become clear to you that there is no baddy in your house,

your room,

or anywhere around you,

even though it **FEELS** like there might be.

Your baddy-thoughts will begin to seem ho-hum.

DULL

BORiNG tiresome

dreary **HO-HUM**

Ho-hum thoughts are like worn-out gum.

Stale.

No longer interesting.

Easy to spit out.

And there is an even better part.

You can use the baddies-are-like-gum trick to help
you with the fear of ANY baddy.

If you were afraid of one baddy, and
you chewed out the scariness so
that one no longer bothers you, but
then a new baddy pops into your
head, you can chew again, and the
scariness will go away.

Each chew makes future chewing
easier.

So, remember your three steps:

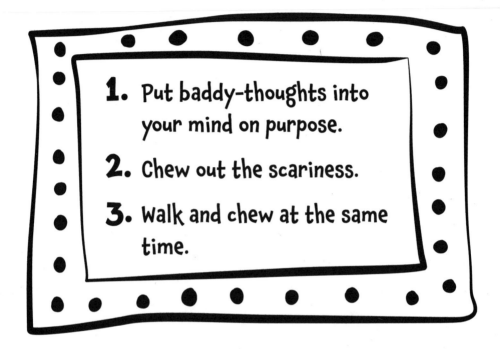

1. **Put baddy-thoughts into your mind on purpose.**

2. **Chew out the scariness.**

3. **Walk and chew at the same time.**

You can do it!

And then you can get on with your life.

There is just one more thing.

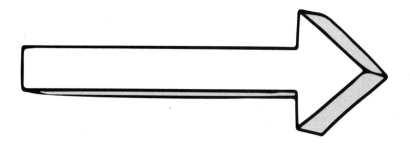

Baddies are often invented by authors and game designers and movie-makers because there are people who LIKE to feel afraid.

Even though you aren't one of those people, you might be interested to know what goes on behind the scenes when scary movies are made. For example:

FUN FACT
The Cowardly Lion costume in The Wizard of Oz weighed 90 pounds. The costume was so complex and the makeup so hard to apply that once he was suited up, the actor was only allowed to eat soup and drink milkshakes so he could stay clean.

FUN FACT
The first actor given the role of the Tin Man in The Wizard of Oz was so allergic to the silver makeup that he had to give up the role.

FUN FACT
The Wicked Witch of the West in The Wizard of Oz was played by a kindergarten teacher whose green copper makeup got so hot during a fire scene that it burned her.

FUN FACT
An animal scientist was so upset about how hyenas were portrayed on The Lion King that he sued the movie studio on behalf of hyenas everywhere.

FUN FACT
The actor in How the Grinch Stole Christmas had a tough time with his costume, too. He was covered from head to toe in green yak fur and had to wear oversize contact lenses that hurt so much they were abandoned midway through the filming.

FUN FACT
Real sharks are hard to tame, and the mechanical shark built for a scary movie about sharks kept breaking during scenes, so the director had to figure out a way to scare viewers without showing a shark at all. He ended up using music, instead.

FUN FACT
The props people for old time movies used chocolate syrup for blood. The movies were made in black and white, so the color didn't matter, and the consistency of the syrup was just right.

FUN FACT
When making a scary movie, sometimes even the actors have a tough time. The cast of one movie used the code word "taco" when they needed to take a break.

FUN FACT
The actors in one scary movie had to ride a roller coaster 26 times in a row to get the final scene right. The first time was probably fun. The twentieth time, not so much.

FUN FACT
The special effects team for one scary movie tested out all kinds of soup before deciding that pea soup looked just like vomit.

FUN FACT
Long ago, painted grapes were used to make scary-looking eyeballs.

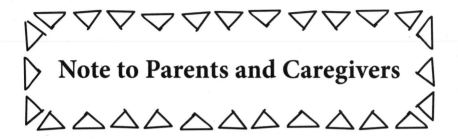

Note to Parents and Caregivers

You want your child to feel safe. To walk around your home and go into rooms alone. To close their eyes after you've said a loving goodnight, and fall gently, mildly, peacefully to sleep.

You want your child to go out into the world confidently. To play and explore without the looming fear of someone snatching them, or something terrible happening. Yet for some children, that isn't the way it is.

Facing Mighty Fears About Baddies and Villains is for children who live in safe houses, on safe streets, in safe neighborhoods, yet still feel afraid of "baddies." Baddy might not be the term you use. You might say bad guy, or monster, or villain. You might use the name of the baddy if there is a particular character your child fears or refer to a category like aliens or ghosts.

Because there are so many kinds of baddies, and because your child does not need to be introduced to new ones in the pages of this book, the general term "baddy" was adopted to cover any feared character—real or imagined—as long as, importantly, the character poses no actual danger to your child.

You have undoubtedly already reassured your child, telling them that the baddy isn't real, or isn't of danger to them. That's great. But if you need to reassure your child every day, it is time for a different approach. And certainly, if your child now avoids being alone, or if they do things like check locks or bury their heads under blankets, they are in need of something more.

There is a loop that forms for anxious children, one that is easy to get started and hard to end. In this loop, your child feels afraid, so they do something self-protective—like ask for reassurance or refuse to go upstairs alone. And then, when the thing they fear doesn't happen, they think, "Whew. It's a good thing I got my dog, or my sister, or my dad, to come upstairs with me." And they mistakenly believe that the actions they took were necessary, when the truth is they were never in danger to begin with.

When you go along with your child's self-protective behaviors, it's like you are saying, "I agree with what you are doing. You really are in danger." That is not the message you want to be sending. Instead, your child needs help moving away from their (unnecessary) self-protective behaviors. That's where *Facing Mighty Fears About Baddies and Villains* comes in.

Read this book with your child. You might read it all at once or spread it out over time. Pause to read the Fun Facts about gum. Why gum? Well, the book is based on exposure, a cognitive behavioral technique that helps children face and ultimately habituate to the things they fear. It turns out that gum is a good analogy for exposure, which helps children "chew out" the scariness baddies. In fact, if you allow gum in your house, you might want to buy a pack to reinforce what your child is learning.

Some additional tips

1. There are baddies in the world, actual people who do hurtful things. Teach your child the basic rules of safety.

2. Not all books, movies, and games are appropriate for children. While inadvertent exposure is beyond your control, do your best to exercise caution around what you allow your child to read, and watch, and play online. Remember that the line between reality and fantasy is slippery for children. Scary images have staying power and are unlikely to fade on their own.

3. Once your child has developed the fear of a particular baddy, and especially if they have adopted self-protective behaviors, avoidance will only make the problem worse. Much as you or your child might want to believe it, out-of-sight does not mean out-of-mind. We cannot run away from our thoughts but instead need to neutralize them. The steps outlined in this book will show you how.

4. Help your child implement all three steps. Exposure is a highly effective technique, although it does require parental support and a commitment to practicing at least 15 minutes a day. Re-read the book as many times as your child needs to hear it. And if you get stuck, check out the Resources section for more ideas.

5. As your child starts "chewing," encourage bravery by saying things like, "I know this feels scary, and I know you can do it." Keep your voice warm and your breathing steady. Your calm

sends a message to the primitive part of your child's brain that is always on the lookout for danger. Make sure you are signaling both safety and confidence in your child.

6. Be aware of your own feelings. If your child's fear annoys you or makes your own anxiety skyrocket, you may need additional support. There's no shame in that. Please seek the help you and your child need.

7. If anxiety—about baddies, villains or anything else—is significantly interfering with your child's life or the life of your family, please reach out to a mental health professional able to guide you in the use of exposure and other tools.

You can do this. Your child can do this. I'll be rooting for you.

Dr. Dawn

Resources

Organizations

These organizations provide information about childhood anxiety, and include therapist locators to assist with finding specialized care:

USA

The Anxiety and Depression Association of America:
https://adaa.org

The International OCD Foundation:
https://iocdf.org

UK

Anxiety UK:
www.anxietyuk.org.uk

Young Minds:
https://youngminds.org.uk

AU/NZ

Beyond Blue:
www.beyondblue.org.au

Kids Health:
https://kidshealth.org.nz

Please also reach out to your child's pediatrician for names of local providers.

Web-based resources

https://library.jkp.com
Dr. Dawn's Seven-Step Solution for When Worry Takes Over: Easy-to-Implement Strategies for Parents or Carers of Anxious Kids, see page 78.
Video Training Course

www.anxioustoddlers.com
Natasha Daniels of AT Parenting Survival creates podcasts, blog posts, and free resources about anxiety. She also offers subscription courses, coaching, and treatment.

https://childmind.org
This NY Institute offers articles on a host of topics, including anxiety, with a unique "Ask an Expert" feature providing trustworthy, relatable advice.

https://copingskillsforkids.com
Janine Halloran provides free, easy-to-implement, child-friendly tips on calming anxiety, managing stress, and more.

https://gozen.com
Kid-tested, therapist-approved, highly effective animated videos teaching skills related to anxiety, resilience, emotional intelligence, and more.

www.worrywisekids.org
Tamar Chansky of WorryWiseKids provides a treasure-trove of information for parents of anxious children.

Recommended reading

The books listed here are Dr. Dawn's current favorites, a snapshot from a particular moment in time. Please also search on your own, or check with your preferred bookseller, who can guide you toward up-to-date, appealing, effective books particularly suited to you and your child.

For younger children

Anxiety Relief Workbook for Kids: 40 Mindfulness, CBT, and ACT Activities to Find Peace from Anxiety and Worry by Agnes Selinger, PhD, Rockridge Press.

Hey Warrior: A Book for Kids about Anxiety by Karen Young, Little Steps Publishing.

Little Meerkat's Big Panic: A Story About Learning New Ways to Feel Calm by Jane Evans, Jessica Kingsley Publishers.

The Nervous Knight: A Story About Overcoming Worries and Anxiety by Anthony Lloyd Jones, Jessica Kingsley Publishers.

What to Do When You Worry Too Much: A Kid's Guide to Overcoming Anxiety by Dawn Huebner, PhD, American Psychological Association.

When Harley Has Anxiety: A Fun CBT Skills Activity Book to Help Manage Worries and Fears by Regine Galanti, PhD, Z Kids Publishing.

For older children

Coping Skills for Kids: Over 75 Coping Strategies to Help Kids Deal with Stress, Anxiety and Anger by Janine Halloran, PESI Publishing and Media.

Help! I've Got an Alarm Bell Going Off in My Head! How Panic, Anxiety and Stress Affect Your Body by K.L. Aspden, Jessica Kingsley Publishers.

My Anxiety Handbook by Sue Knowles, Bridie Gallagher, and Phoebe McEwen, Jessica Kingsley Publishers.

Name and Tame Your Anxiety: A Kid's Guide by Summer Batte, Free Spirit Publishing.

Outsmarting Worry: An Older Kid's Guide to Managing Anxiety by Dawn Huebner, PhD, Jessica Kingsley Publishers.

Superpowered: Transform Anxiety into Courage, Confidence, and Resilience by Renee Jain and Shefali Tsabary, PhD, Random House Books for Young Readers.

Take Control of OCD: A Kid's Guide to Conquering Anxiety and Managing OCD, 2nd Edition by Bonnie Zucker, PsyD, Routledge Press.

For parents

Anxious Kids, Anxious Parents: 7 Ways to Stop the Worry Cycle and Raise Courageous and Independent Children by Reid Wilson, PhD, and Lynn Lyons, LICSW, Health Communications Inc.

Breaking Free of Child Anxiety and OCD: A Scientifically Proven Program for Parents by Eli R. Lebowitz, PhD, Oxford University Press.

Freeing Your Child from Anxiety, Revised and Updated Edition: Practical Strategies to Overcome Fears, Worries, and Phobias and Be Prepared for Life by Tamar Chansky, PhD, Harmony.

Growing Up Mindful: Essential Practices to Help Children, Teens, and Families Find Balance, Calm, and Resilience by Christopher Willard, PsyD, Sounds True.

Peaceful Parent, Happy Kids: How to Stop Yelling and Start Connecting by Laura Markham, PhD, TarcherPerigee.

The No Worries Guide to Raising Your Anxious Child: A Handbook to Help You and Your Anxious Child Thrive by Karen Lynn Cassiday, PhD, Jessica Kingsley Publishers.

The Yes Brain: How to Cultivate Courage, Curiosity and Resilience in Your Child by Dan Siegel, MD, and Tina Payne Bryson, PhD, Bantam Press.

Dr. Dawn's
SEVEN-STEP SOLUTION FOR WHEN WORRY TAKES OVER
Easy-to-Implement Strategies for Parents or Carers of Anxious Kids

worry has a way of turning into WORRY in the blink of an eye. This upper-case WORRY causes children to fret about unlikely scenarios and shrink away from routine challenges, ultimately holding entire families hostage. But upper-case WORRY is predictable and manageable once you understand its tricks.

This 7-video series will help you recognize WORRY's tricks while teaching a handful of techniques to help you and your child break free.

Each video contains learning objectives and action steps along with need-to-know content presented in a clear, engaging manner by child psychologist and best-selling author, Dr. Dawn Huebner. The videos are available from https://library.jkp.com.

Video One: Trolling for Danger (time 8:15)

- The role of the amygdala in spotting and alerting us to danger
- What happens when the amygdala sets off an alarm
- Real dangers versus false alarms
- Calming the brain (yours and your child's) to get back to thinking

Video Two: The Worry Loop (time 10:15)

- The "loop" that keeps Worry in place
- How to identify where your child is in the Worry Loop

Video Three: Externalizing Anxiety (time 11:41)

- Externalizing anxiety as a powerful first step
- Talking back to Worry
- Teaching your child to talk back to Worry
- Talking back without entering into a debate

Video Four: Calming the Brain and Body (time 13:36)

- Breathing techniques
- Mindfulness techniques
- Distraction techniques
- Which technique (how to choose)?

Video Five: Getting Rid of Safety Behaviors (time 15:18)

- Preparation
- The role of exposure
- Explaining exposure to your child
- Creating an exposure hierarchy

Video Six: Worrying Less Is Not the Goal (time 13:02)

- The more you fight anxiety, the more it holds on
- The more you accommodate anxiety, the more it stays
- Anxiety is an error message, a false alarm
- When you stop letting Worry be in charge, it fades

Video Seven: Putting It All Together (time 19:42)

- A review of the main techniques
- Deciding where to start
- The role of rewards
- Supporting your child, not Worry